Taking Photos from Space

Rane Anderson

D1306793

✳ Smithsonian

Contributing Author

Allison Duarte, M.A.

Consultants

Tamieka Grizzle, Ed.D.
K–5 STEM Lab Instructor
Harmony Leland Elementary School

Valerie Neal
Curator and Chair of the Space History Department
Smithsonian

Publishing Credits

Rachelle Cracchiolo, M.S.Ed., *Publisher*
Conni Medina, M.A.Ed., *Managing Editor*
Diana Kenney, M.A.Ed., NBCT, *Content Director*
Véronique Bos, *Creative Director*
June Kikuchi, *Content Director*
Robin Erickson, *Art Director*
Seth Rogers, *Editor*
Mindy Duits, *Senior Graphic Designer*
Smithsonian Science Education Center

Image Credits: front cover, p.1, pp.4–5 (all), p.7 (insert), p.10 (right), p.13 (insert), p.16, p.20 (all), p.25 (all), p.26 (top) NASA; pp.2–3, p.26 (bottom), p.27 U.S. Geological Survey; pp.6–7 Planet Observer/UIG Universal Images Group/Newscom; p.11 Science Source; p.12 (insert) Dmytro Gilitukha; p.15 (top, both) © Smithsonian; p.18 RadioFan; p.21 GE Astro-Space Division/Science Source; p.23 (insert) Eric Albrecht/The Columbus Dispatch via AP; all other images from iStock and/or Shutterstock.

Library of Congress Cataloging-in-Publication Data

Names: Anderson, Rane, author.
Title: Taking photos from space / Rane Anderson.
Description: Huntington Beach, CA : Teacher Created Materials, [2018] | Audience: K to grade 3. | Includes index.
Identifiers: LCCN 2017056320 (print) | LCCN 2017061737 (ebook) | ISBN 9781493869251 (e-book) | ISBN 9781493866854 (pbk.)
Subjects: LCSH: Landsat satellites--Juvenile literature. | Photographic surveying--Juvenile literature. | Cartography--Remote sensing--Juvenile literature.
Classification: LCC TL798.S3 (ebook) | LCC TL798.S3 A53 2018 (print) | DDC 526.9/82--dc23
LC record available at https://lccn.loc.gov/2017056320

Smithsonian

Teacher Created Materials

5301 Oceanus Drive
Huntington Beach, CA 92649-1030
www.tcmpub.com

ISBN 978-1-4938-6685-4
© 2019 Teacher Created Materials, Inc.

Printed in China
Nordica.042018.CA21800320

Table of Contents

Superhero Vision

Would you like to be a superhero with superhuman vision? You could spot a disaster from miles away. You could stop a forest fire. You could put an end to starvation and drought. Well, you might not be a superhero. But you could still do all those things with the help of a series of satellites called Landsat.

These satellites have infrared vision. That means they can see heat. And that helps them see things that humans cannot. From space, satellites take photos of Earth's surface. Then, scientists study the photos. They compare them to images that were taken weeks, months, or even years before. They look for signs of trouble. If they find any, a team of scientists and engineers starts brainstorming ways to fix it.

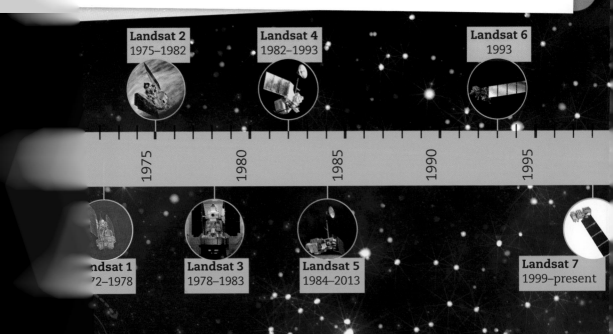

Landsat 2
1975–1982

Landsat 4
1982–1993

Landsat 6
1993

1975   1980   1985   1990   1995

ndsat 1
'2–1978

Landsat 3
1978–1983

Landsat 5
1984–2013

Landsat 7
1999–present

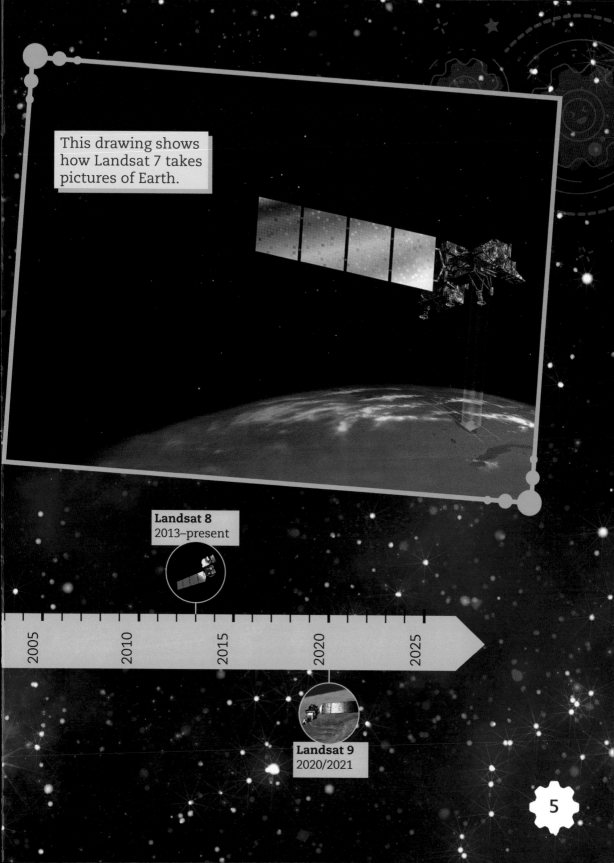

This drawing shows how Landsat 7 takes pictures of Earth.

Landsat 8
2013–present

2005　2010　2015　2020　2025

Landsat 9
2020/2021

The Big Picture

Imagine your nose pressed up to a painting. What do you see? Odds are, you cannot describe the painting in much detail. You are too close to the canvas to see the whole picture. Some things, such as paintings, make more sense when viewed from a distance. With your feet on the ground, you are very close to Earth's "canvas." From the ground, you can learn a lot about the world. But the world is a big place, and you are only seeing a small part of it. Some things on Earth are too difficult to understand without taking a step back.

Remote sensing does just that. It gives views of Earth from high above the ground. It uses satellites in space or high-flying aircraft to make images of Earth's surface. It allows scientists to see a big part of the planet at one time. That helps them make big discoveries.

San Diego, a city in California, looks very different from land (left) than it does from space (above).

There are many satellites that orbit Earth collecting data.

Before remote sensing, people had to get creative to take a picture of Earth from the sky. They attached small cameras to balloons, kites, and even pigeons!

Make Some Waves

The sun shines on Earth from space. What do you feel when you are outside on a sunny day? The sun makes your body warm. And it helps you see everything around you. Heat and light are two forms of **electromagnetic radiation**. These waves of energy and light are what make Landsat images possible!

There are many types of radiation that come from the sun. **Visible light** is the type people can see. **Infrared light**, felt by most people as heat, is a type of light people cannot see. Scientists use both to study Earth from space.

Both types of light move in waves. Imagine that you tie a piece of string to a chair. You hold the other end and flick your wrist up and down. The string moves in waves. You can move it faster and slower. This will make different **wavelengths**. Light and heat move in waves just like the string. Landsat sensors can measure the length of waves. Some are tiny, and others are miles long.

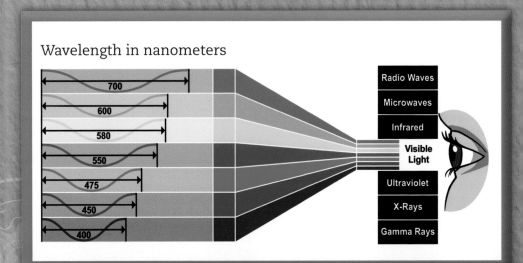

Wavelength in nanometers

700
600
580
550
475
450
400

Radio Waves
Microwaves
Infrared
Visible Light
Ultraviolet
X-Rays
Gamma Rays

This photo shows how a lighthouse would look in ultraviolet light, which can't be seen by the human eye.

Wavelengths

Scientists classify light by measuring the length between its waves. Violet light has the shortest waves that we can see. Red light has the longest. The infrared light has a wavelength that is even longer than red. Sensors on Landsat collect these lengths as data. The data help make infrared images.

Landsat's Eyes

Sunlight looks white, but it is actually a mix of all colors. Each color has its own wavelength.

Think about sunlight that hits a stop sign. The stop sign absorbs all the colors of light but red. The red light then **reflects** off the stop sign, and you see red. All objects on Earth absorb and reflect light and heat.

Landsat's sensors are like eyes that stare at Earth from space. The sensors scan Earth. They measure wavelengths that reflect off the surface. In a sense, each object on Earth has its own heat "fingerprint." A healthy plant will reflect certain wavelengths. A sick plant will reflect other wavelengths. Landsat can notice these differences. That data can be used to make an image.

white light

red surface

Red light reflects off a red surface and other colors of light are absorbed.

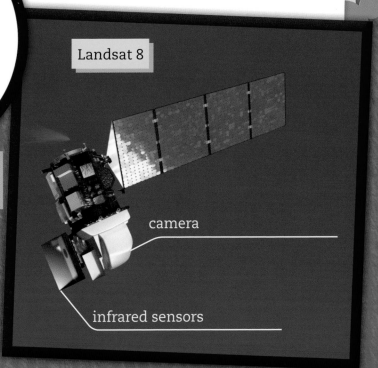

Landsat 8

camera

infrared sensors

In this image of the United States, red shows where grass, trees, crops, and other plants are growing.

A Light Experiment

Try this experiment to see how light works. Hold a basketball in the sunlight. You should see the color orange. Now, take the ball into a room that is dark. What do you see? Without light, you cannot see the color of the basketball. That is because there is no light to reflect off the ball.

Seeing the Problem

The world has come to rely on Landsat images. They are used all over the world by all kinds of people. They are even used to solve real-world problems.

Fiery Disaster

Forest fires are scary things. They can burn thousands of acres and destroy hundreds of homes. Land managers try to prevent them. Some of their methods are risky. They set fire to parts of forests. These are called **controlled burns**. Some of these "controlled" burns get out of control. They turn into real forest fires. In many cases, these fires do more harm than good. Land managers needed a better way to prevent fires.

Dry and dead plants catch fire easily and burn quickly. So forests with a lot of dry and dead plants are at the greatest risk. Landsat images can help land managers find dry parts of the forest. Then, they can focus their fire prevention on those spots.

A firefighter uses a controlled burn to prevent a big fire.

This picture of a wildfire in Arizona was taken by Landsat 7.

Eagar

Greer

Nutrioso

Alpine

Apache National Forest

Hannagan Meadow

LANDFIRE is a fire prevention program. It relies on Landsat data to find where fires are likely to strike.

Farming Feat

A farmer's **livelihood** depends on healthy crops. But sometimes, crops get sick. A farmer might not find out until it is too late. After all, crops can take up thousands of acres of land. There is no way a farmer can check each and every spot on a regular basis.

Who has time for that? Landsat does!

In just one image, a farmer can check the status of each crop. The image can show different kinds of information. It can show whether crops are healthy or diseased. A farmer can see whether crops have pests. He or she can even see if part of a crop is flooded. When compared with other pictures, Landsat can show changes in crops over time.

This photo shows a healthy forest.

1

Two months later, the same forest has been destroyed by pests.

2

gypsy moth

Color Pop

The colors in infrared images seem to jump right off the page. This is done to highlight important parts of the images. Contrasting colors stand out. Red shows healthy parts of a forest. Green shows parts of a forest destroyed by gypsy moths. Red and green are contrasting colors. At just one glance, it is easy to tell what is going on.

Underwater Forests

Most forests on Earth are easy to spot. But what about when the forest grows on the ocean floor? Giant kelp forests do just that. They grow near the coasts in cool ocean water around the world. Kelp is important. It is a major source of food and shelter for many sea animals.

Scientists wanted to learn more about kelp forests and how they grow over time. Kelp forests are easy to see from above. They look like small green dots out in the blue ocean water. So scientists collected thousands of images from Landsat. But they ran into a problem.

There were way too many pictures to look at. It would be fastest to use computers. But the computers could not tell the difference between kelp and sea foam. Scientists had to find a way to filter the images without a computer.

Scientists asked the public for help. They put all the pictures on a website. People went online and marked where they saw kelp in Landsat images.

kelp

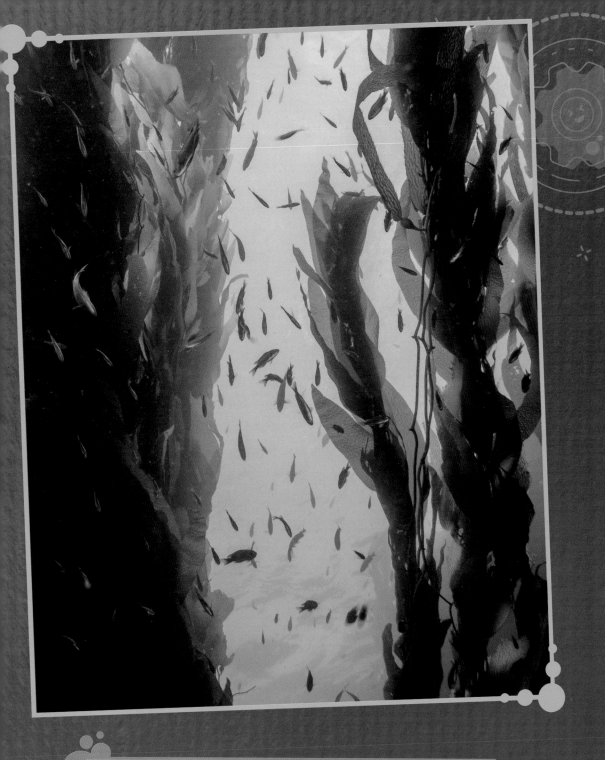

Kelp can grow 46 centimeters (18 inches) in one day.

The Landsat program has had much success. It has changed the way people see the world. But it has had some setbacks along the way. Sensors failed. Radios failed. A satellite got lost. Scientists and engineers learned from these setbacks. They came up with new ideas that shaped the future of the program.

Landsat 4

Less than one year after its launch in 1982, Landsat 4 had a lot of problems. It lost the use of two of its four solar panels. And the main and backup downlink transmitters both died. That meant Landsat 4 could not talk to Earth. But it could talk to other satellites. So NASA launched a relay satellite the next year. Landsat 4 could now send its data to the relay. Then, the relay could send it to NASA stations on Earth.

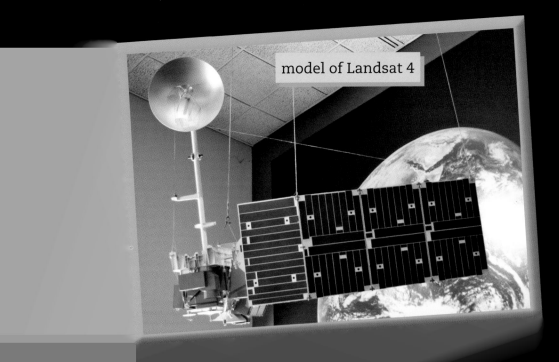

model of Landsat 4

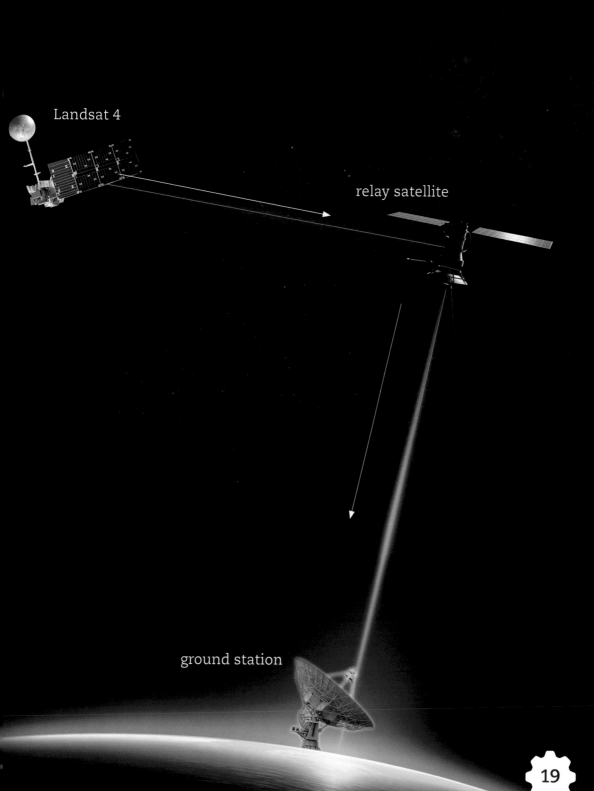

Landsat 4

relay satellite

ground station

Landsat 6

Landsat 6 launched in 1993. But it never made it into orbit around Earth. The pipes that took fuel to the **stabilizers** failed. It did not travel very high into the air after its launch. Instead, it fell back out of the sky. Millions of dollars and the hard work of thousands of people were lost.

Engineers had to fix the problem. First, they had to find out what went wrong. Sensors on the rocket recorded a large jolt right before Landsat 6 split from the rocket. A jolt at that time and place meant one thing: there was an explosion in the fuel valve.

As a result, engineers had to think of a new way to make the fuel system. They needed to find a simple design that would not break. After many tests, they did it.

An engineer works on Landsat 7

drawing of Landsat 6

ENGINEERING

Built to Last

To design a new fuel valve for the next Landsat, engineers had to think about what a valve must do. Valves had to open when needed and stay closed at all other times. They must stay closed through a hot, rough rocket launch. They must stay closed in the freezing void of space. Then, they must open when told to and not stick, jam, or explode. Engineers had to test valve designs until they made one that worked!

Algae Blooms

Farmers use fertilizer to help their crops grow. Sometimes they use too much. A lot of it gets washed away by rain. This **runoff** then collects in rivers and lakes. There, it makes **algae** grow in large "blooms." These blooms float on top of the water. They block sunlight from getting below the surface. This hurts plants and fish that live in the water. The algae also release toxins into the water. These toxins can make people sick.

Lake Erie is a water source for millions of people. But the water is not always clean enough to drink. In 2014, algae blooms were so bad that people were told not to drink tap water for three days.

In the past, algae blooms in Lake Erie got out of control because of **phosphorus**. This chemical can be found in fertilizer. But people had worked to fix that problem for decades. Runoff from farms was lower than in the past. So why were the blooms worse than ever?

Drainage water often brings toxins with it.

Ducks paddle through a large algae bloom.

The algae in Lake Erie comes to the shore.

Landsat to the Rescue!

Scientists found a new method to measure the blooms in Landsat images. They went back into the Landsat 5 **archive**. They pulled up about 30 years of old images of the lake. Then, they used the new method on the old images. This helped scientists see the algae problem in a new way.

It turns out that over time, phosphorus had settled into the sand and dirt at the bottom of the lake. Most of the time it was buried, so it did not mix with the water. But at times, the phosphorus in the sand and dirt was uncovered and it mixed into the water. This brought the algae blooms back. The mystery was solved! The good news is that the lake will return to normal over time. That is, as long as the runoff stays clean.

Algae blooms in this pond because of runoff from a nearby fertilized field.

This picture of an algae bloom on Lake Erie was taken by Landsat 8.

Landsat 5 is listed in *Guinness World Records* as the "longest-operating Earth observation satellite." It operated for 28 years and 10 months.

The Next Generation

The legacy of the Landsat series will carry on. In 2020, the ninth model is set to launch!

NASA is still haunted by the loss of Landsat 6. The old model 5 was in orbit alone for six years. That was a dangerous time. Landsat 5 could have shut down. That would have cut off the world from the satellite's data.

NASA wants Landsat 9 up and running as soon as possible. To save time and money, Landsat 9 will become Landsat 8's twin. Their designs will be almost the same. But Landsat 9 will have some upgrades. It will be able to take more than 700 images of Earth a day. Landsat 8 can only take 550 images. The twins will team up. They will pass over the same places, but at different times. So one of the two satellites will pass over the same spot on Earth every eight days! That means more data and more updates. And that means more chances for Landsat to come to the rescue!

These Landsat images show Hurricane Harvey as it moves and then stops over Texas in 2017.

Index

Do you want to study Earth?
Here are some tips to get you started.

"People who monitor weather, disasters, natural resources, and land use rely on Landsat images. But it's not just scientists who look at these pictures. Chances are, you have used them, too! Have you ever used Google Maps? Landsat images are used for many mapping programs." **—Jim Zimbelman, Geologist**

"Some Landsat data is available to everyone for free! You can find information about the program on the NASA and United States Geological Survey websites. There are many ways that people use Landsat images and data. This information is great for scientists who study the environment!" **—Andrew Johnston, Research Associate, Center for Earth and Planetary Studies**